GIANT AFRICA

CW00924557

The Best Guide On Everything You
Need To Know About
Caering,Breeding,Housing Of
Giant African Land Snail

Mathew Anthony

Table of Contents

CHAPTER ONE

GIANTAFRICAN LAND SNAIL BEHAVIOR AND TEMPERAMENT

These tremendous snails are steady omnivores, and have been known to bite through mortar dividers (hypothetically on the grounds that they contain follow measures of calcium, which snails need for shell wellbeing).

Luckily, they're not carnivores. They are, in any case, incredibly strong, which is the reason endeavors to destroy them has been troublesome.

Notwithstanding their ravenous hungers, many individuals in the U.K. also, Asia keeps these snails as pets, portraying the snails as having adorable appearances and expressive eyes.

Giant African land snails are bisexuals, which mean they have both the female and male conceptive organs. Two snails are as yet required for reproducing, yet they are exceptionally productive raisers. A folic can apparently lay 1,200 feasible eggs each year, with a few hundred eggs in a solitary grasp.

In case you are keeping giant African land snails, you should be very cautious about discarding the various eggs created. Pervasions of giant African land snails can be a huge danger to native vegetation pretty much anyplace the creatures live.

LODGING THE GIANT AFRICAN LAND SNAIL

A decent measured, all around ventilated plastic or glass tank with a protected cover is needed for this species. For only a couple completely mature snails, you would require a 5-to 10-gallon tank.

Bits of wood, plug bark, or dirt vases give a fascinating scene and concealing spots for the snails. The substrate should be wiped out week after week. Fog the tank every day to keep the substrate marginally clammy (not wet, nonetheless). Snails need consistent dampness to forestall parchedness and shell issues.

In spite of the fact that they come from a heat and humidity, monster African land snails appear to adjust well to bring down temperatures. The tank temperature would should be somewhere in the range of 70 and 77 degrees Fahrenheit, so you would need to utilize heat strips, which will expect you to focus better on the dampness. What's more, in case you are warming the enclosure, it will dry out quicker, so you should ensure the mugginess is kept up with.

FOOD AND WATER

Giant African land snails eat almost continually in nature. Their eating regimen incorporates generally vegetables and natural products. They're not predatory; however they are omnivores, so they will eat nearly anything. Snails need calcium to keep their shells solid and, notwithstanding a wellspring of promptly accessible calcium, they have been known to bite through mortar dividers, which gives follow measures of the mineral.

These snails get heaps of dampness from their food yet may require a bowl of water, intended for reptiles with the ventured edges to hold the snail back from siding into it. Be ready to clean the bowl oftentimes.

CHAPTER TWO

NORMAL HEALTH PROBLEMS

Like different snails, giant African land snails are inclined to aestivation, which happens when it's in a walled in area or climate that is excessively dry. At the point when this occurs in bondage, the snail frames a layer over the kickoff of its shell and seals itself inside, concealing the charming, inquisitive face that makes it a decent pet, and expecting you to fog and screen the warmth near bring it back out.

Snails likewise are helpless to pervasions of parasites and flies.

While most such bugs are minimal in excess of an annoyance and can be disposed of via cautious washing, a few parasites can tunnel into the snail's body and make it lazy and awkward.

Giant African land snails need a wellspring of calcium to keep their shells solid. While a snail can self-fix minor breaks in its shell, a few breaks might allow its body to stay uncovered, which might prompt parchedness.

Most extraordinary pet veterinarians in the U.S. won't treat giant African land snails since they are unlawful.

BUYING YOUR GIANT AFRICAN LAND SNAIL

You can't lawfully buy this creature in the United States. In case you're found attempting to carry one into the country you could be fined by the United States Department of Agriculture. Notwithstanding, on the off chance that you find one and carry it to the consideration of the USDA, the organization is probably going to be thankful for the help and you will not be punished.

DEALING WITH

These snails don't appear to mind being taken care of, yet you should be delicate with them and try not to harm the shell. Saturating your hands prior to holding them is suggested by certain proprietors.

The shell is generally delicate at the base where it is close to the body, so attempt to try not to get them by this piece of the shell, and be mindful so as to offer strong help to the body and shell.

It's a smart thought to wear gloves in case you will deal with a goliath African land snail; the creature's sludge, or seepage, is accepted to contain parasites poisonous to people. Continuously wash your hands completely subsequent to taking care of a snail.

IS IT LEGAL TO OWN A PET GIANT AFRICAN LAND SNAIL?

Because of the danger of turning into an effective obtrusive animal types and being a genuine agrarian bug, importation of giant African land snails into the United States isn't allowed, and it is unlawful to keep them as pets in the U.S.

COMPARATIVE PETS TO THE GIANT AFRICAN LAND SNAIL

In case you're keen on a pet like the land snail that is more accessible, look at these choices:

- Mantis Shrimp

- Land Hermit Crab

- Tokay Geckos

- Emperor Scorpion

The giant snail originally from East Africa, the giant African land snail (Achaia folic), has been set up all through the Indo-Pacific Basin, including the Hawaiian Islands. Since 2011, these snails have been found in Miami, Florida. Albeit the current reach is restricted toward the southern scopes of Florida, this snail can withstand freezing and go into hibernation for as much as a year.

This permits them to all the more effectively grow their reach toward the north, particularly during long periods of hotter winters. This snail is types of worry because of its serious level of intrusiveness and its capability to hold onto zoometric microbes. African land snails are known to be the host of different types of parasites and microbes; including yet not restricted to the rodent lungworm (Angiostrongylus cantonensis) and (Salmonella enteric). They additionally are known to devour more than 500 types of plants and represent a food security hazard, particularly given the huge horticulture industry in Florida. Lee town Science Center analysts are considering ideal approaches to test for the presence of the rodent lungworm on this species just as leading a populace hereditary qualities concentrate on this species.

REACH AND DISTRIBUTION

Giant African land snails are local to East Africa and found in Asia. In the USA, in Southern Florida and Hawaii, the snails are under isolate. The USDA APHIS (Animal and Plant Health Inspection Service) has set up extra managed regions in Florida (June 2015). The snails are sold and brought as pets up in different nations, including those of Europe. While not yet in New York, the goliath African land snail, inferable from the illicit pet exchange, is disallowed in the state.

CHAPTER THREE

One of the biggest earthly snails, totally mature grown-ups can arrive at right around 8 inches (20 cm) long and 5 inches (13 cm) in breadth. Grown-up shells are earthy with hazier brown longwise stripes, have seven to nine whorls including an enlarged long body whorl, and cover a large portion of the length of the snail. Snails have female and male regenerative organs. One mating can bring about various grips of eggs over the long haul. Fast populace increments are reasonable on the grounds that each snail can deliver 1,200 eggs each year.

HOSTS AND HABITATS

The snails are found in many plant environments and are known to specially devour beans, peas, cucumbers, melons, and peanuts. Likewise in danger are decorative plants, tree husk, and surprisingly the mortar, plaster, or paint on structures.

EFFECTS

Due to their huge size, capacity to burn-through more than 500 various types of plants and cause harm to mortar and plaster structures, the giant African land snail is quite possibly the most harming snails on the planet. The snails are likewise a possible danger to human wellbeing since they can convey a parasitic nematode that can cause meningitis.

ANTICIPATION AND CONTROL

Giant African land snails can endure cold temperatures in a semi-hibernation state. They address an expected danger to New York despite the fact that they flourish in tropical/subtropical regions. In the event that a snail shell is bigger than two inches (5-6 cm) it is in all likelihood a kind of giant snail. Try not to deal with exposed hands. Importation is denied and examples will be seized by customs. Try not to buy as pets or as instructive creatures through unfamiliar online sellers or neighborhood merchants. For safe evacuation, or on the other hand whenever discovered outside or available to be purchased, contact neighborhood New York Department of Environmental Conservation, Cornell Cooperative Extension, or USDA workplaces.

REARING

All snails are bisexuals, which imply that they have both male and female sex organs, so in spite of the fact that you need two snails with the end goal for them to raise, it doesn't make any difference which two. In case conditions are great, the snails will create homes of little, white round eggs. These ought to be eliminated cautiously, so the grown-ups don't upset them, and set in a little holder containing some soggy sans peat substrate, where they should bring forth after around 14 days at 20-25°C. Watch out for your eggs, and when they incubate give them some food and cuttlefish.

Snails can create more than one grasp of eggs following mating. Therefore, snails that have not have been in touch with different snails for quite a while may in any case deliver groups of feasible eggs (accepting the snail was a grown-up when it was in touch with different snails).

TAKING CARE OF

The African Land Snails are extremely simple to take care of, as they will eat a wide assortment of things. The best food is lettuce and cucumber yet apple, banana and cabbage can likewise be given. Notwithstanding, in the event that you give your snails food that goes off rapidly (like banana and apple) make certain to eliminate it when it has gone brown so as not to make your snails sick. A fundamental piece of the snail's diet is calcium. This is utilized to keep their shells solid and sound and calcium can be given as a cuttlefish bone.

CHAPTER FOUR

LODGING

These snails can be housed in an assortment of holders, contingent on the size and number of snails that you have. A decent holder is a glass or plastic aquarium tank. These kinds of compartments permit simple cleaning and you will actually want to watch your snails through the sides. The snails like to tunnel, so when you have your tank, fill it with a few centimeters of sans peat manure and an enormous piece of bark. (On the off chance that you gather the bark yourself ensure that you absorb it water for the time being to eliminate any dreadful synthetic compounds). Ensure that the substrate is kept wet consistently, however not spongy. Leaf litter and greenery are likewise acceptable at keeping the dirt soggy. The tank ought to be kept at 20-25°C, which implies that a little warmth mat or cushion is important throughout the cold weather months. The tank ought to be kept clammy and a plant shower is great, furnishing it hasn't been utilized with synthetics as these could hurt your snails.

In case snails are not kept in right conditions they might seal the gap (opening) to their shell and trust that conditions will improve. In the event that this happens you should ensure you are keeping the snails accurately. Whenever you have settled these lodging issues you can urge the snails to open up again by washing them in Luke-warm water.

WELLBEING AND NEATNESS

Giant Land Snails ought to be treated with a similar consideration and thoughtfulness regarding tidiness as some other pet. In the same way as other creatures (confined birds, snakes, reptiles, turtles, reptiles and so forth) and some food items (crude poultry and eggs), snails can convey the Salmonella microscopic organisms.

Therefore, subsequent to taking care of snails (or clearing them out), you should wash and sanitize hands altogether.

PARASITES

The AES is sporadically gotten some information about parasites conveyed by Giant African Land Snails. In the same way as other slugs and snails, Giant African Land Snails are equipped for conveying a parasite known as Rat lungworm (Angiostrongylus cantonensis). This is a parasite of rodents however the hatchlings is passed to snails when snails eat contaminated rodent droppings. Rodents then, at that point eat the snails and the parasite is passed back to the rodent to finish its life cycle.

This parasite can be passed to people in the event that they eat live/crude tainted snails or a piece of a snail. As a rule disease doesn't need clinical treatment be that as it may, in exceptionally uncommon cases, can cause an uncommon type of meningitis.

THE END

Printed in Great Britain
by Amazon

66168316R00020